T0198516

LOVE VERSES

AVIS VERONICA SIMMONDS

To order additional copies of this book, contact:
Xlibris
844-714-8691
www.Xlibris.com
Orders@Xlibris.com

ISBN: Softcover   978-1-6641-3854-4
        EBook   978-1-6641-3853-7

Print information available on the last page

Rev. date: 10/22/2020

DEDICATION

Love is in the air, and our family is full of cheer. Therefore, I dedicate this book to Kenneth Conrad Spencer Simmonds, my firstborn child who got married, January 2020, to his beautiful, awesome Lady, Lieutenant Anitra Denise Highland. Importantly too, I dedicate this book to our newborn grandson, Xavier Langston Karter Simmonds, my second grandchild. These family events are all wrapped up in love and therefore, this book, *Love Verses* is so appropriate at this time of my writings.

As I write, I will always think of my Mother, Dorothy Agatha Tatem Williams Harris, who gave me all the love a mother gives her infant child – care, protection, nurturing; in other words, giving me all the light she had raising me on the beautiful island of St. Kitts, in the Caribbean. To my sisters and brothers, peace and love.

To my husband Dr. Keith Cecil Simmonds, my eternal love and friend, the love of my life; the joys of life, as we celebrate 50 years of togetherness in September, 2020. Thank you for taking care of me and your Three fabulous children, Kenneth, Gwendolyn and Kevin. You allowed me to rise high and fly like a beautiful butterfly, up, up and away. Thank you!

Introductory Page

 Lavish me in the aroma of lavender

 Overflow my bouquet with petals of petunia in the colors of love

 Venture into my loving arms. Have no fear, it's a journey of unfolding mysteries, with flickering lights like the Aurora Borealis, illuminating our love

 Eternity is our destiny, wait for me if you arrive before me; I will be raptured in your love!

LOVE VERSES

My son fishes in the pond as a child; but my love fishes for me where the sun sets on the golden pond. We are in love!

Pedrick Crossing Drive, Tallahassee, FL.
My son fishing at age 9. Photo by Yours Truly

Photo by Yours Truly.
Black Rock Seaside, St. Kitts, West Indies

As strong as these rocks against many storms, so is my love for the love of my life and we'll whither life's storms, because love is kind, gentle, understanding and most of all, long suffering.

An aunt's look of love as she thoughtfully watched over her nephew. He will grow up to give her his love in return.

The sunrise lights up the day to guide my love to my home, where there is peace and joy overflowing with love

Photo by Yours Truly.
Pedrick Crossing Drive, Tallahassee, FL

The creeping purple bell could not bear to be fenced in alone; so will my love come creeping over the fence to take me away to his love land.

Photo by Yours Truly

Photo by Yours Truly.
Pedrick Crossing Pond, Tallahassee, FL

Am dreaming in the park, that the trees will change their reflection and show me the reflection of my love that am dreaming of, for he walks tall and upright as the trees; and I await his presence, because I am in love with this man!

I will follow my love wherever he leads me, even down to the water's edge. Water refreshes!

Photo by Yours Truly.
Cascade Park, Tallahassee, FL

The flaming skies, set the tone for love; let me melt in your arms my love from your tender touch!

Photo by Yours Truly.
Pedrick Pond, Tallahassee, FL

In the early morning mist, I feel the chill in the air that reminds me of the chills I get from the touch of my love's gentle hands caressing me. I am so in love!

Photo by Yours Truly.
Pedrick Crossing Drive, Tallahassee FL

Photo by Yours Truly.
Pedrick Crossing Drive, Tallahassee, FL

Her grandfather's love will follow her not only in the backyard, but all through her life.

I sat in the yard, lonely as the banana tree, waiting for my love to walk by and capture me.

Pedrick Crossing Drive, Tallahassee, FL.
Photo by Yours Truly

St. Kitts-Anguilla-Nevis Reunion, Nevis, 2018.
Photo by Yours Truly

"If music is the food of love, play on …" But Caribbean steel pan music! It rocks one's soul and makes one fall in love with a man she is dreaming all about.

To win the heart of my love, I was told that good food is the way to his heart and soul, then a walk down the isle of the church. He said: "I do, I do love you!"

Friendship and reunion at an island breakfast,
St. Kitts, West Indies, 2018.
Photo by Yours Truly

The island of St. Kitts, Kittian Hill, 2018.
Photo by Yours Truly

I will climb any mountain, even on suspended bridges to reach my love, because I hear his voice calling me from the valley below, and I must find him.

He took me under the apple tree shaded from the sun, then he shared with me the fruit of his land, the love of his hand. My Brother-in-Law's fruit garden. St. Kitts, West Indies 2018

Southeast Peninsula, St. Kitts, West Indies, 2018.
Photo by Yours Truly

I traveled the winding roads and across mountain terrain in search of my love, then as I reached the seashore, he waived goodbye in his fishing boat, but he'll come back for me, he is mine!

Her love came surfing on the waves to take her across the seas on his surfboard where his ship was anchored, and they sailed away to love land.

Hawaii Beach, 2017.
Photo by Yours Truly

Hawaii, 2017.
Photo by Yours Truly

They drifted away from their men on the shore and beckoned them to bring them ashore on their love boat, the surfboard. Lovers they are!

My love is as spotless as this island flower in bloom, and I give him my love, he is all I need to keep me secured.

Photo by Yours Truly.
Hawaii Botanical Garden, 2017

Polynesian Cultural Center, Hawaii 2017.
Photo by Yours Truly

Like the waterfall, am falling in love in nature's garden, so serene, captured in awe with my love

Take me in your hand as a beautiful flower, protect me from the sun and drench me with your water of love, my love, and let me bloom eternally! I am yours!

Botanical Garden, Hawaii 2017.

Pedrick Crossing Pond, Tallahassee, FL.
Photo by Yours Truly

He walks across bridges in the setting sun, he knows he will find his love before darkness descends. He walks and walks, for she too is walking, looking for her love. They will find each other for they are so in love on a healthy walk.

Black Butterfly spread your wings of beauty, take me along to find my love who awaits me yonder in his garden of love. He is a Black Stallion, my love!

Pedrick Crossing Drive, Tallahassee, FL
– Photo by Yours Truly

Traveling from Vancouver, Canada, by train.
September, 2017. Photo by Yours Truly

I will sit in the shadows of the evening and await my love. I need my love!

Take me across your bridge of love, sale away with me on calm waters, hear the echo of my voice from the mountain top, shouting: I am yours and you are mine, Come to me my love!

Vancouver, Canada to Seattle, Washington 2017.
Photo by Yours Truly

Traveling through the Country Roads of Georgia, 2018.
Photo by Yours Truly

On Georgia country road, I travelled all alone in search of my love. I have no fear of crossing county lines to find him, for he is mine and mine alone!

My heart is ablaze with love for the lover of my life, like the image of the blazing cloud in the sky, majestically hovering the land where lovers meet and melt in its heat. Am all inflamed for my love!

Photo by Yours Truly.
Pedrick Pond, Tallahassee, FL

Traveling along Georgia country roads, 2018.
Photo by Yours Truly

The cotton trees transformed into my wedding gown, as I married the love of my life, the man in my life forever and throughout eternity; he is mine!

She is beautiful in Pink like the Pink flowers beautifying the landscape. Then comes her lover man in silk with silk flowers; he wants to keep her forever as his treasure!

The wild-flower patch, Thomasville, Georgia
Summer 2018

Flight to Atlanta, GA 2018.
Photo by Yours Truly

As the plane glides through the clouds, the golden sun will light up the evening shadows as I welcome my love into my world when he lands.

I waited for my love, as his plane flies between heaven's beautiful skies of nimbus clouds. And on my billows of breasts, he will land and be at rest!

Flight to Atlanta, Georgia, 2018.
Photo by Yours Truly

*Taken by Yours Truly. At the
Dublin's house in Virginia, 2018*

Roses are Red Violets are Blue,
Yellow is true as I look for my
fellow, will he be in Blue? He
loves me too!

True friendship lasts forever in love, over Fifty years. Sharing life joys of family, watching our children and grandchildren grow up in love, peace, understanding of their world and embracing the human race in love.

My friend Eunie of over 50 years.
Summer 2018

I sailed from island to island with the love of my life. I kissed his face under the rising sun as I looked at him in the early morn. We are lovers forever!

Cruising along the Caribbean Seas, 2018.
Photo by Yours Truly

Take me to the waters, let us drink of nature's flow. Then, let's dive into the pond and ascend renewed in love! And when winter is gone, let us Spring in love forever.

Pedrick Crossing Pond, Tallahassee, FL.
Photo by Yours Truly

Cascade Park, Tallahassee, FL 2019.
Photo by Yours Truly

Shadows of the evening steals across the sky and brought calm, peace and love, to lovers in the park.

I will take a seat and wait on my love; he will meet me in the park. The evening colors of the sky sets the tone to wait for my love. What is the color of love?

Cascade Park, Tallahassee, FL 2018.
Photo by Yours Truly

He lights up my life like the heavenly lights; I will follow him all around in the daylight.

Pedrick Crossing Drive, Tallahassee, FL,
Photo by Yours Truly

The Falcon has come to take me away. Now open your wings oh Falcon bird, take me up high as you fly. My love awaits me beneath the Northern Lights where I will find him there with delight.

Backyard of Pedrick Crossing, January 2019

Photo by Yours Truly

The winter rose has company with the berries and a blooming bud, reminding me of the companionship I have with my love at my side, keeping me warm on a winter's night

I arose in his arms as the sun rises in the Eastern skies. My day will be shining, bubbling with love from the love of my life

Pedrick Crossing Drive, Tallahassee, FL.
Photo by Yours Truly

Pedrick Crossing Drive, Tallahassee, FL.
Photo by Yours Truly

Natures beauty in Pink, reminds me of the Lady in Pink. She is loved and is graceful as the rising sun clouds of pink, floating on air in the early dawn. We will fight with her, for her, stand by her until there's a cure. She is a Lady in Pink and is loved. In Honor of Breast Cancer Month.

And when the dark clouds appear, shelter me from the oncoming storm; should it rain, wash me with your feathery hands, then take me away protected by your love, my love!

Photo by Yours Truly

Pedrick Crossing Drive, Tallahassee, FL.
Photo by Yours Truly

I sat on the roof top mesmerized by the floating fleecy clouds. I am dreaming about the love of my life as he flies through the heavens on wings like a dove to bring me tidings of his undying love. Then as the gentle, chilling breeze touched by brow, I look down and there he was smiling up at me. I am in love!

Like rain drops on the flower, saturate me with your oozing sweat, while I lay my head on your chest and slumber in your arms to rest. You are my love!

Pedrick Crossing Drive, Tallahassee FL 2019.
Photo by Yours Truly

Pedrick Crossing Pond, Tallahassee, FL.
Photo by Yours Truly

My love shines his love all over me, like the firey sun rays that heats my heart feeling his tender, burning touch. Am in love!

I will follow the jet streams crossing the skies to find my love, and I will have my arms wide open for him to land, so he can feel my tender touch. He is my love!

Pedrick Crossing Pond, Tallahassee, FL

Sister and brother share a vacation trip with love, because family matters; family is where love begins and is taught.

Brother and Sister, St. Kitts, the Caribbean, 2019

The Renes are all locked up in love, tied up in locks and will be forever one, because they are in a world of love, so in love!

Tallahassee, FL 2019.
Photo by Yours Truly

We have loved for over 50 years, since September, 1970, and together we will always be in love and make it through COVID-19 year 2020; Soul mates throughout eternity.

Leeds, England 2013

Cousins love at a tender age will last forever and they will grow up in family love together.

Grandpa's glow of love for his grandson lightens up the room. He was born into a family, a model for his life.

He is cradled lovingly in his uncle's arms; a model in his life as he grows into manhood in the Simmonds arena of life.

My son and his newborn son, born March 7, 2020. So protected a child in this COVID-19 year. His father's guidance will protect him all through his years, and his mother's love will follow him everywhere. A family in love! Salute the Newly Weds!

I will follow my love to the depth of the ocean, for he is my rainbow guiding my pathway to find him; and I will love him in all the colors of the rainbow, because love is beautiful.

Photo taken by Drexel Glasgow in the British Virgin Islands, the Caribbean, on October 12, 2020

When life, love and your caressing hands are no more, like the tree resting into the earth, lay me gently into the arms of Mother Earth to a peaceful rest, where I will await you. You have been my Earthly love!

Photo by Yours Truly. Pedrick Crossing Drive, Tallahassee, FL

Printed in the United States
By Bookmasters